The Extra Money Machine:

Make Money On Top Of Money With PayPal

R.A.Franklin

First and foremost, thank you for your support and making my efforts put forth to create this book, worthwhile.

In this book, I will show you the method I use to generate additional money through Paypal. There are no mysteries or uncertainties, if you're able to get a PayPal account in your region, you're willing to utilize PayPal Savings, and you qualify for at least the PayPal Debit Card, you too can earn money on top of money with Paypal.

STAGNATION FRUSTRATION

I began exploring and experimenting with additional opportunities due to my growing frustration with the stock market. Additionally, I believe in diversifying my investments rather than putting all my eggs in one basket. While some stocks can be shooting stars, they might eventually burn out and crash. Other stocks may be slow and steady, but they still carry the risk of slumps. The gains can be significant if you catch the right wave, but most people can't afford to gamble with uncertainty because money doesn't grow on trees. Let's be honest, not everyone has time to watch those waves all day unless they're a day trader with a significant amount of money they're willing to risk. The average person can't afford to play with tens of thousands of dollars, so I wanted to come up with an alternative.

I won't portray the stock market as entirely doom and gloom because it has its benefits if you know what you're doing. Therefore, I won't be making comparisons throughout this book. However, I will say that the approach you're taking here doesn't come with the same risks, and you will earn extra money that doesn't require selling anything, talking to anyone, or investing.

That said, let's proceed and set up your PayPal account!

RODERICK A. FRANKLIN

SIGN UP FOR PAYPAL

To sign up for a PayPal account, follow these simple steps:

1.) Go to the PayPal website in your web browser.

2.) Click "Sign Up."

3.) Choose between a Personal or Business account (Personal is used for this Book).

4.) Enter your email address and follow the instructions.

5.) Provide your personal or business details and create a password. (Expect to include your banking information, also include your primary debit card details.)

6.) Follow the on-screen prompts to complete your account setup.

Once done your account has been set up, you're officially ready to send, receive, and manage money securely with PayPal! This is a vital part of the process.

LET'S ADD PHONE VERFICATION FOR BANK TRANSFERS

Now that your account has been created, increase the security. Make sure to save your login info in a secure location. Some of you prefer to auto save passwords
in your Google or Windows accounts, which is fine, but let's increase the security of your account even further by setting up phone verification.

To confirm your phone number for PayPal account purposes, follow these steps:

1.) Log in to your PayPal account through a web browser.

2.) Click on the Settings icon next to "Log out."

3.) Under the "Phone Numbers" section, click + Add New (or Change next to the phone number you want to confirm if you're updating your number).

4.) Enter the phone number and select the phone type.

5.) Click Add phone number.

6.) Choose either "Text you a code" or "Call you to confirm".

7.) Enter the confirmation code and click Validate.

This process ensures that your phone number is verified for secure money transfers, which gives you peace of mind and adds another lock to your safe!

Speaking of safety: Avoid using unknown, unsecure, or public wifi connections. We never know who has access to the data or what they may desire doing with it. Use personal, trusted wifi or your own cellular data.

SIGN UP FOR PAYPAL SAVINGS ACCOUNT

Now that you've set up that extra layer of security for your account, lets set up your PayPal Savings account!

To set up a PayPal Savings account, follow these steps:

1.) Log in to your PayPal account.

2.) Locate the "Finances" tab and click or tap it.

3.) Select the "Savings" tab.

4.) Follow the prompts, which will guide you through opening a PayPal Savings account and provide terms and conditions.

The beautiful thing about this, is that you won't need a minimum deposit! Just keep in mind that having something in the savings account, allows you to earn interest from it.

This is another vital component, and at the time of this book being written, the APY for PayPal Savings is 4.3%.

For those unfamiliar with APY: APY (Annual Percentage Yield) represents the total interest earned on an investment over a year, including both the nominal interest rate and the effects of compounding. It's a more accurate measure of the true return on your investment compared to the nominal interest rate.

Sure, simply utilizing PayPal savings, will allow you to make money while saving money, but we're taking things a step further to increase the pace.

THE EXTRA MONEY MACHINE

SIGNING UP FOR A PAYPAL DEBIT CARD

Now to get your PayPal Debit Card. These are the steps to sign up for a PayPal Debit Card is a straightforward process that allows you to access your PayPal balance conveniently.

To apply for the PayPal Debit Card, follow these steps:

1.) Log in to your PayPal account.

2.) Navigate to the PayPal Debit Card page.

3.) On the PayPal home page, go to the "Wallet" section.

4.) Look for the option to apply for the PayPal Debit Card.

5.) Click on "Request your card" and follow the on-screen instructions.

6.) You will need to provide some personal information and confirm your mailing address.

7.) Verify your information and submit your application.

- No credit check is required since this is not a credit card.

The benefit to utilizing the PayPal Debit Card is the 5% cashback based on a specific category of your choice that's decided on each month. You can decide whether that category should be groceries, gas, restaurants, clothing, and the list goes on. If you're going to be spending big in a certain category during a certain month, make that your category for the month.

If the category each month maximizes out your earnings, that's even better because you get 5% back on up to $1,000 per month from the debit card.

Extra money earned with this debit card is $50/month or $600/year. This is money earned without additional efforts. This could actually help with your budget if you keep things consistent by way of transferring a set amount to your PayPal account to make required purchases in a certain category. Grocery shopping is one of the most consistent purchases I can think of, and depending on the amount you spend on a monthly basis this could be the category for you. I wouldn't recommend spending just for the sake of cashback though, it's all about benefitting from your everyday purchases that were going to occur anyway.

Don't forget the 4.3% APY you'd benefit from on that $600 when you place it in your PayPal Savings. That's $625.80 that gives you a better idea of what you can do with the extra money machine! This is money on top of money being made with a little extra effort, but it doesn't stop there if you desire earning more. If so, let's move forward in terms of signing up for the PayPal Credit Card.

SIGNING UP FOR A PAYPAL CREDIT CARD (OPTIONAL)

Now for the optional step in setting up your "Extra Money Machine", which is applying for the PayPal Cashback Mastercard. This step is completely optional because it gives you additional cash back if you choose to
use it for the remaining expenses you have to cover within the budget under the limit your card has.

To apply for the PayPal Cashback Mastercard, follow these steps:

1.) Log in to your PayPal account through a web browser (not the PayPal app).

2.) Click on the Settings icon next to "Log out."

3.) Under the "Phone Numbers" section, click + Add New (or Change if updating your number).

4.) Confirm your name, address, phone number, date of birth, annual income, and the last 4 digits of your Social Security number.

5.) Proceed after reading the Terms and Conditions, if you agree.

6.) Link the card to your PayPal account (it was automatically linked for me and yours should be linked as well).

Now you're all set to start earning cash back on all purchases! Let's dive into what you will be doing, and (hey) no worries, it's a simple process but it is a process that you will have to work, in order for it to work for you.

The PayPal Cashback Mastercard gives you the ability to earn 3% cash back when you check out with PayPal and 1.5% on all other purchases everywhere the card is accepted.

HOW TO USE YOUR EXTRA MONEY MACHINE

Now that you have your money machine set up, here's how you use it:

PayPal Debit Card: Choose the particular purchase category you'd like to go with each month.

If a single purchase is going to be close to $1000 or more and it falls within one of the designated categories, go with that category to use your PayPal Debit Card for the month. This helps max out the cash back rewards you
can nab for the month with the debit card. If the category better serves you by way of groceries, go with that category. It could actually help you in regards to your budget if you aim to stick to a certain amount. $1000/month in groceries can be quite a bit of food for some people, while on the other end some households spend $250/week on groceries with ease. You can either transfer the $250/week over to your PayPal account to reserve for that expense or make sure that your PayPal Debit Card can take the money out of your Bank account if the money in your PayPal account isn't enough to cover the expense.

You get a stronger handle on your spending if you transfer the amount over, especially if you want to keep an eye on the budget.

There isn't much to this, but here are the steps to transfer money and how to select your category:

To transfer money from your bank account to PayPal, follow these steps:

A.) On the Web (PayPal.com):

- Go to your Wallet.

- Click Transfer Money.

- Choose "Add money from your bank or debit card."

- Enter the amount and select either "In seconds with debit (which is usually free)" or "In 3-5 days with your bank."

B.) On the PayPal App:

- Tap "Add Money" beside your balance.

- Select "From your bank or debit card."

- Enter the amount and choose either "In seconds with debit" (recomended) or "In 3-5 days with your bank."

Remember that there are daily, weekly, and monthly limits for transferring money to your PayPal balance from your bank. You can add up to:

- $5,000 USD per day

- $10,000 USD per week

- $20,000 USD per month

To select the PayPal Debit Card cash back reward category, follow these steps:

A.) Log in to your PayPal Account.

B.) Access your Account Settings:

- In the app, tap on the "Accounts" tab.

- On the website, navigate to your account setting.

C.) Choose your Monthly Cash Back Category:

- Look for the option labeled "Choose your monthly cash back category".

- Select this option to view the available categories.

D.) Select your Preferred Category:

- You will see a list of categories such as groceries, gas, restaurants, clothing, and health and beauty.

- Go with the one that you will utilize the most, based on your monthly expenses.

E.) Confirm your selection:

- After selecting your category, tap "Next" or "Confirm".

- Review the category offer details and tap "Got it" to finalize your choice.

PayPal Cashback Mastercard: You don't have a max earning limit on a monthly basis with this credit card, but you do have your credit card limit. If you limit the costs to your necessities based on your budget, you win.

If you stick to your limit, which I will say is $1500 for example and that money is transferred over to your PayPal account to cover the needs as reflected in your budget, it will help you earn cash back monthly while paying off the balance immediately. The money is there, so it would allow for you to immediately remove the risk of unnecessary fees. Don't wait until the last minute, sometimes you may feel tempted to use the money for something else because credit cards do buy time before the bill comes due, but consider it a flame you're leaving unsupervised with the risk of it turning into a major fire. Put it out immediately in order to protect your Extra Money Machine if you choose to use a credit card.

To transfer money from your bank account to PayPal, follow these steps:

A.) On the Web (PayPal.com):

- Go to your Wallet.

- Click Transfer Money.

- Choose "Add money from your bank or debit card."

- Enter the amount and select either "In seconds with debit (which is usually free)" or "In 3-5 days with your bank."

B.) On the PayPal App:

- Tap "Add Money" beside your balance.

- Select "From your bank or debit card."

- Enter the amount and choose either "In seconds with debit" (recomended) or "In 3-5 days with your bank."

Remember that there are daily, weekly, and monthly limits for transferring money to your PayPal balance from your bank. You can add up to:

- $5,000 USD per day

- $10,000 USD per week

- $20,000 USD per month

VISUAL EXAMPLES

PREVENTATIVE MEASURES

If you can't pay it immediately because there is no balance showing, just make sure to pay it as soon as a credit card balance emerges with all the money you've transferred over to your PayPal balance. This keeps things under control.

* Regardless of whether a balance shows on the credit card or not, if you've made purchases, it will show in the recent activity so that you atleast know what you need to transfer from your bank to PayPal. This helps simplify the math and prevents you from losing track. Transfer the money ahead of time according to your budget or the same day to avoid the charges turning into a headache in terms of tallying up the total. Once the balance appears under the "PayPal Cashback World Mastercard" category (just scroll down on the Home tab on the web or to the right of the app), make the payment.

<u>To make a payment to your PayPal Credit Card using your PayPal balance, follow these steps:</u>

1.) Under the "PayPal Cashback World Mastercard":

- Click "Make a Payment".

- Select the "Current balance" amount.

- Click "Next".

2.) Under "Choose a way to pay":

- Choose "PayPal Balance".

3.) Confirm Payment Details.

4.) Complete the Payment:

- Confirm the payment by clicking "Pay".

- You will receive a confirmation message once the payment is successful.

Remember that there are daily, weekly, and monthly limits for transferring money to your PayPal balance from your bank. You can add up to:

- $5,000 USD per day

- $10,000 USD per week

- $20,000 USD per month

Now that you understand how to use your Extra Money Machine, let's get into the best part, the extra money!!!

THE PAYPAL PAY OFF

The PayPal Pay Off will come in the form of the cash back rewards in addition to the 4.30% APY in your PayPal Savings:

PayPal Debit cash back rewards:

Extra money earned with the debit card is $50/month or $600/year which is 5% cashback with the $1000 monthly cap.

Extra money earned with the credit card is $45/month or $540/year which is 3% cashback of a $1500 credit card limit with PayPal checkout. There is no earnings cap beyond your available limit.

Extra money earned with the credit card is at least $22.50/month or $270/year which is 1.5% cashback of a $1500 credit card limit where Mastercard is accepted. There is no earnings cap beyond your available limit.

* **Again, I wouldn't recommend spending just for the sake of earning cash back, it's all about benefitting from your everyday purchases that were going to occur anyway.**

The pay off doesn't stop there, because you will be taking these cash back earnings and placing them right in your PayPal Savings where the 4.3%APY awaits.

To give you an example of what your 4.3% APY can produce in a year based on the cash back you've deposited, we will use two of the amounts listed above:

PayPal Debit 5% Cash Back $600 + PayPal Credit 3% Card Cash Back $540 = $1140

Factor in the 4.30%APY = $1,189.02 for the year

Not bad for money you didn't have to go out and earn, right? Great news, it doesn't stop there, because you can use the Extra Money Machine in anyway you please:

- If you choose to spend the extra money regularly, that's a personal choice that can result in extra money to be used where needed. May the cash back rewards serve you well.

- If you choose to save the extra money earned, this can bring larger rewards to impact you even more at a later time thanks to the interest.

*** Use your points, don't lose your points. If you don't earn at least 10 points using your PayPal account within 1 year's time (365 consecutive days) or complete at least three eligible paypal transations you run the risk of losing your points. Any points should be cashed out as money to your Paypal account anyway so they can earn you money within your Paypal savings, but this warning has been added so that money doesn't go down the drain.

Overall, think of what your extra money machine can do for your life in the years to come.

Thinking long-term, 5, 10, or even 20 years down the line, this approach is a fantastic way to help your adult children earn extra money and assist them with their financial future by creating their own machine. It doesn't stop you from working either; remember, it's the "Extra Money Machine." The extra income can alleviate stress during emergencies, unexpected layoffs, or paying off lingering debt, further boosting your ability to save money.

It can also fund a nice trip, and if you reach a certain amount, the interest can help with monthly bills. This could even open the door to living comfortably in a country with a lower cost of living, with minimal to no work if your annual interest more than covers your annual cost of living. This is especially beneficial for those with retirement in mind and don't want to spend their elderly years clocking into a job, but starting early makes this easier to accomplish. Consider using it in combination with other options if you have access to other high yield savings accounts, CDs and things of this nature. CDs are for those with long term savings in mind.

What I mean by using your extra money machine in combination with other accounts, is to consider transferring some or all of your extra money gained. This will allow you to transfer it to a different account with a higher APY to benefit from if there are no fees and penalties you object to. If this motivates you to add money to your savings account from your paychecks, even better if you can afford to do so.

This book was created to deliver a simple option to earn additional money while impacting our lives in a positive way, and I hope it truly impacts yours for the better.

Consider a budget, living within your means, saving up for wants, and this should give you more room to breathe with less stress. Enjoy your Extra Money Machine!

See More:

Paypal Rewards Program Agreement

ABOUT THE AUTHOR

R. A. Franklin

Roderick grew up in a single-parent household with his mom, siblings, and cousin. Determined not to be a financial burden on his mother, he found creative ways to earn money from a young age to fulfill his childhood wants. In elementary school, he would salvaged flowers from a florist to sell in front of a local gas station, hiring friends to help them earn money as well. In middle school he sold candy in between classes through a deal with a local store owner that required no out-of-pocket expense. These are a few examples, but Roderick's entrepreneurial spirit has always driven him to find innovative solutions to assist himself and others financially at various age ranges.

In school, math became a fun challenge for Roderick as he discovered various paths to solve problems. He also helped fellow classmates increase their understanding of math and science assignments. His high school math teacher, who considered leaving the school, was persuaded to stay after Roderick spoke to his classmates about the benefits of respecting and appreciating her dedication to their understanding and success. With their sights set on graduating, they went on to improve their performance and behavior in class. Roderick's high school math teacher is now retired and also attended his wedding years after highschool. His high school grades reflected his proficiency, and he also graduated with a Bachelor of Science honors degree in college.

With this book, Roderick aims to share practical steps for others to make extra money without taking on additional hours at a job or more financial burdens. He is excited to have your support and hopes to make a positive impact on your lives and financial stability. He is confident that the steps outlined will allow everyone to earn back the cost of this book in less than a month, and then some.

www.ingramcontent.com/pod-product-compliance
Lightning Source LLC
Chambersburg PA
CBHW030046230526

45472CB00005B/1702